Singing 101

Vocal Basics and Fundamental Singing Skills For All Styles and Abilities

Nancy Bos

Reissued January 2017, Revised May 2018 and December 2020 by StudioBos

ISBN: 9781520354415 ASIN: B01N35UAXW

DEDICATION

To my husband and kids for their love and support.

CONTENTS

Nancy Bos

ACKNOWLEDGMENTS

Special thanks to Stacey, Alice, and Samantha for their help bringing Singing 101 to life.

My deepest gratitude goes to those singing teachers who most influenced my path to writing Singing 101: Robert Edwin,
Dr. Candace Magner, Dr. Scott McCoy.

Additional thanks to all of the other wonderful voice teachers I've studied with over the decades: Alan Stanga, Dr. Monty Barnard, Helen Houden, Dr. Stephen Parker, Julian Patrick, Ute Freund.

FREE singing exercises to strengthen and tone your voice at:
NancyBos.me/media

1 INTRODUCTION

Singing is a great part of being human! Everyone should get to sing freely without judgement or hesitation. That's a lot to ask! But each one of us has just as much right to express ourselves through singing as anyone else.

That's why it is important that you are investing your time and energy to improve your singing, and this book is a very good start. Combine working on the lessons in this book, especially using the 21-Day Action Plan and Journal, with free exercise tracks available on my website, nancybos.me/media.

We are not all blessed with equal talent. And very few of us have the obsession that it takes to make it big and be a famous singer. But we should all get to enjoy singing whenever we get a chance.

The first thing you need to know is what a voice teacher is. The second thing you need to know is what this book is. A Voice Teacher is someone who can teach you how to use your voice to the best of its ability – that's not a coach. A Voice Coach works with you to prepare a performance for a specific type of music, to make it sound convincing or to perform it well so your audience enjoys it. In this book, I am not a voice coach; you won't work on any specific type of music. I'm not going to work with you on pop, rock, country, classical, whatever. I am here to give you a foundation in how to sing better no matter the kind of music you like.

This book contains voice lessons on crucial topics; essential information to help you think of singing in a new way. This book is not just a bunch of vocal exercises. It is not a quick fix, a short cut, or a guaranteed road to success. What this book is, is top-notch foundational voice study. It is founded in science. It is a great, detailed start; techniques to rely on for all singing. It will give you an excellent start in your vocal study. If you are an experienced and skilled singer, a lot of this information will be a valuable review.

After you've completed this book, seek out a talented teacher to take one-to-one lessons. I am serious about this. It is so important to get a trained set of ears and an experienced observer to guide learning. It is also the most cost-efficient way to become a better singer. Ask music people in your area for referrals, or go through a great organization called the National Association of Teachers of Singing – that is NATS.org, or talk to community college or university music departments. Look for someone who specializes in the type of music that you like to sing – or at least enjoys the type of music you like to sing. The basics are pretty much the same for any style, but after you get the basics down, you'll want a teacher who understands your style. Consider this book to be a foundation to prepare you for when you are ready to find that private teacher.

Take full advantage of this book. It is packed with information on breathing, posture, resonance and tension.

- Breathing: Opening up your torso to allow air in, controlling the collapse of your torso while letting air out.
- Posture: What physical alignment allows for the best sound for your voice instrument?
- Resonance: Controlling the type of sound that comes out of you; whether it is a country western sound or a big opera sound; that's mostly resonance.
- Tension: Be in charge of how much tension you allow for the sound you want. Don't tip your chin up on high notes. Don't bunch your

tongue up in your mouth when you're saying your "r's". There are many more hidden tensions to uncover.

Practice the exercises in this book over and over again. Understand them in your head and your body. Break old habits. Start forming better habits.

Finally, before you begin, make sure you are in a room where you can practice these exercises with freedom of movement (you're going to have to lie down for parts), and be in a place that allows for the mental freedom you need to make all kinds of different sounds.

Enjoy! I know these lessons will benefit you in many ways.

2 BREATH BASICS

Here is an unusual way to think about the mechanics of singing; singing is the controlled release of air past two membranes in your throat. That's all it is; releasing air at a controlled pace past two little vocal folds in your throat. If you can use your breathing muscles to control the air coming through your voice box (aka larynx) you will be able to control your pitch, energy, and length of phrase.

In order to really understand the concepts in each chapter, we will do one or more activities in each. For Breath Basics you will need room to lie down on your back. You will elevate your knees so that your lower back is comfortable, but if you would like to put a pillow under your knees instead, or add a pillow under your lower back, that is fine.

Some of the activities will involve making lots of sound. But this one is all about breathing without much sound. We will focus on how our bodies feel when we breath, and progress to how our bodies feel for other sounds, including singing.

Activity

1 Lie down on the floor on your back. Bend your knees comfortably with your feet on the floor. Put your hands on your belly and take a nice, deep, calm breath.

2 Do you feel your belly rise when you breathe in? This low breathing is the type of breathing we do when we are sleeping. It is a very efficient way to take a breath. Try it again and check out your shoulders. Are

they moving? Probably not – they sure don't need to. Relax your shoulders to the floor.

3 Although it may feel a little false, I want you to laugh; a big Santa Claus laugh (Ho, Ho, Ho). Do you feel the tension in your abdomen when you do that? That is the tension we can use to control air coming out.

4 Now try an evil, nasty little laugh like a wicked witch. Even more tension? That is a very basic form of what some voice teachers call "breath support." The tension is your breathing muscles controlling the release of air.

5 Next take in a deep breath. Fill your lungs completely with air, allowing your abdomen to rise, and release it on a long musical sigh on pitch, going from the top of your range to the bottom.

6 Try it one more time, but this time, while you're releasing that air, don't let your rib cage collapse and sink in so fast. Take your time. Try to keep your rib cage wide, expanded, to release the air at a controlled pace. One way to think of this is to imagine if you had your hands holding everywhere around your rib cage and abdomen, and instead of letting your ribs and abs go in, your hands are able to keep your core wide and big like a column. This expansion, or tension, around the width of your rib cage is another part of your breathing muscles controlling the release of air. Here we go. Let's fill up – and sigh. Was that controlled? That's better.

That's the type of controlled release of air that we use when we're singing.

To review, you were controlling the release of air. You should have felt that control shared to some degree between your belly or abdominal area and the muscles of your lower rib cage. Here's where you should not feel it. You should not feel your shoulders go up. You should not feel your sternum go up like a soldier (Your sternum is the bone between your ribs over the middle of your chest) If you were to do this standing, you should not stretch taller when you breathe in – you should get wider! And you should not get shorter when you sing out – you should - very, very slowly - get narrower.

> *TIP*
> *If you are inclined to have iron abs and always appear as lean as possible, you are going to have to get past that for good singing. You must be willing to let go of abdominal tension and expand around the waist and ribs to get a good breath.*

3 BREATHING IN, BREATHING OUT

We can learn a lot about breathing when we are lying on the floor. But breathing while horizontal is simpler than when we are standing. It also seems to be easier to mentally focus on the breath and body. But singing while horizontal isn't a luxury we get very often. Occasionally singers on the stage are asked to perform stretched out in a bed, but for most of us, we won't get the chance.

Let's give this breathing a try standing up. You'll find out how your rib cage and abs interact the most efficiently for you when you have a vertical experience with the previous horizontal exercise. It will feel quite a bit different. When our ribs plus the weight of our head, arms, and shoulders are stacked on top of our abs it changes our natural breathing. There are a few different ways that a person can breathe "well" for singing. Depending on body type and muscle tone, it might feel better to use more rib cage expansion, or abdominal expansion, or share the expansion equally between the two. Now is your chance to find out what is right for your unique body.

Activity #1

It's time to try the activity from the previous section standing up!

1 Stand with feet shoulder width apart. Put your left hand on your belly and your right hand just below the right armpit. Inhale using a full, rich breath.

2 Do you feel your belly go out when you breathe in?

3 Check your shoulders. Are they moving? Probably not – they sure don't need to. Relax your shoulders down and back.

4 Let's try that big Santa Claus laugh (Ho, Ho, Ho). Do you feel the tension in your abdomen when you do that? That is the tension we can use to control air coming out.

5 Now try an evil, nasty little laugh like a wicked witch. Even more tension? The tension is your breathing muscles controlling the release of air.

6 Next take in a deep breath. Fill your lungs completely with air, allowing your abdomen to get bigger. Your abs need to expand out to make room for your full lungs. Release the breath with sound on a long musical sigh on pitch, going from the top of your range to the bottom.

7 Try it one more time, but this time, while you're releasing that air, don't let your rib cage collapse and your abs sink in so fast. Take your time. Try to keep your rib cage wide, expanded, to release the air at a controlled pace. Imagine if you had your hands holding everywhere around your rib cage and abdomen, and instead of letting your ribs and abs go in, your hands are able to keep your core wide and big

like a column. This expansion, or tension, around the width of your rib cage is another part of your breathing muscles controlling the release of air.

Activity #2

Let's start to refine this a little for singing. This next activity is very similar. But while you are doing it, focus on how this might feel for singing. Breathing like this brings a feeling of power, confidence, and relaxation; all things a performer must have.

1 Put your hands on your abdomen and give out a big sigh; you know, the good kind with control over the release of air. Maybe you felt your shoulders rise when you inhaled and fall when you exhaled. Don't do that when you sing! You'll lose too much control.

2 Next when you inhale feel your abdomen and rib cage expand. As you exhale, feel your abdomen and rib cage go back in slowly. Inhale (expand), and exhale. Now that is a nice, low, deep breath.

3 This next time, fill up your rib cage very wide. Can you imagine that; filling the rib cage up so that it stretches and expands, so that your ribs get wider? You become a huge giant by the time you imagine your rib cage expanding like this.

4 Think about your abdomen expanding by relaxing. As you exhale on a nice long sigh, keep your rib cage wide for as long as possible. Inhale (expand), and exhale. Great! If you got that, very good! Now that is controlling the release of air. This is the habit to get into for great breath for many different singing styles

5 Repeat this exercise several times each day. To remind you, set an alert on your phone. It takes many repetitions to make a new habit. How fast do you want to learn to be a better singer? That's how you will know how often to do this breathing method so it becomes a habit.

6 You might have noticed that the word diaphragm hasn't appeared once so far. There is an old saying to "sing from your diaphragm." But ever since we've been able to do MRIs (starting in the 1970's) on live, breathing people, we've known that this pre-science phrase is at best misleading and confusing, and at worst sets a student up for failure. We are asking them to do something that is actually physically impossible, because the diaphragm is active when we take air in, not when we breath or sing the air out.. As you've already found from these simple activities, breathing for singing is much more complicated than pointing to where one muscle is, and saying, "sing from there." So no need to "sing from your diaphragm" any more. Rather, sing from the core muscles that you have found optimize your breath control!

4 BREATHING WHILE SINGING

In the previous chapters, we did a little bit of inhaling and a little bit of exhaling. Now let's spend more time on the details of inhaling when you are really singing. You can do this breathing and sighing until you get dizzy and fall over – and your body will probably thank you for the deep breathing. But here is where we apply this to singing. Before you start ANY song, even if you are just singing for fun for yourself, you have all of the opportunity you need to take a controlled, relaxed, and beautiful breath; you don't need to gasp the air in!

Activity

We start the initial breath of a song by first expanding the abdominal area, then the lower rib cage, and then the upper rib cage – no, not your shoulders - the upper rib cage under the armpits!

- Abdominal area expands
- Lower rib cage expands
- Upper rib cage expands
- Notice your back
- Let the air go (exhale)

We'll do it again;

- Abdominal area expands
- Lower rib cage expands
- Upper rib cage expands
- Notice your back
- Let the air go (exhale)

More than half of your rib cage is around your sides and back. When you breathe like this, can you feel your ribs expand when you inhale? All the way around your back - Yes! Do you feel your entire torso expand like a column? Get wide! Exhale and try it again. But, if you start to feel dizzy, sit! Put your head between your knees and breathe normally until you are not dizzy anymore. The more you do this the more tolerance you will have for oxygen.

Think you can do this for every breath when you are singing? Nah, probably only in the spots where you have a big rest. But you know what? You have to make this kind of breathing a habit when you sing. You don't want to think about it; you won't have time to think about it in a song. You just have to do it.

> *Watch yourself sing in a mirror*
>
> - *If your shoulders rise, break the habit*
> - *If your abs stay stiff as a board, get out of that habit*
> - *If your body does nothing: if your body does nothing then your singing is probably doing nothing, and you need to add some energy to what you are giving your listeners*

Activity Review

- Breathe in to expand your lower abdomen.
- Continue breathing in to expand your rib cage all around. Feel your back flare like a cobra.
- Add Singing: pick a pitch – any one pitch. Make your mouth into a relaxed open vowel like an "awe." Sing it out
    - Slow!
    - Loud!
    - Controlled!

- Alright, try it again; air in... and sing! And again; air in... and sing!

Yes! I bet that feels great!

Now take a break from this exercise for a few minutes and check in with your brain and body. Make sure you aren't overdoing it and breathe normally for a little while. Believe me; we are just getting started on controlled exhales.

5 THIRTY-SECOND HISS

We are going to spend a little more time controlling the exhale with the idea in mind that everyone needs to sing long phrases on one exhalation. In normal speech we rarely go more than five seconds between breaths, and when we are not talking, our breathing cycle takes between two to five seconds. But for singing, sustaining an exhalation for seven or more seconds is quite common. For this activity we will over-prepare in order to really gain the skill of controlled exhalation.

Activity

In just a minute you will take your great breath in. When you release the breath it will be slowly and quietly on a hiss. Try for a steady hiss, not choppy. This is a time-trial. Your goal is to hiss for 30 seconds – that's a very long time. Find a way to time yourself. When you are ready and relaxed, fill up with air.

- Inhale
  - abs wide
  - rib cage proud and strong
  - breathe deep and wide
- Hold Briefly
  - start the timer
- Exhale
  - and hiss (quietly and gently)

Great! Was that 30 seconds? Wow, seems like an eternity when you are doing this. Maybe you can already hiss for 30 seconds. And certainly some people do have bigger lungs than others. But even the smallest adult body should be able to accomplish this with control and overcoming your instinct to panic, unless there are health issues.. To control the release of that air you are going to control your rib cage coming back in. When you take that deep breath; first to your abdomen, then to your lower rib cage and upper rib cage, start to hiss and try to keep your rib cage and abs expanded as long as possible. And here's a hint, right around 23 seconds, my brain starts to send panic signals. So then I move around just a little bit while I'm hissing. I take a few steps or stretch my arms or something. That distraction really helps me get through to the end.

Here we go again. Inhale and hiss. Relax your jaw while you're doing this, don't let your jaw tighten up. Sternum up

– don't sag!

Did you make it for the full 30 seconds? I hope so. Some people do, some people don't. But hey, be proud of yourself! This is a strange and difficult thing. Keep trying a few times each day until you reach that goal. This extremely controlled release of air seems to be unique to singing and breath based instruments like flute and trumpet. If you haven't used this control with singing or with another instrument, don't expect to get it right away. It is going to take time to develop. Be patient and give yourself time. Because really, making a good sound is mostly controlling the release of air.

6 MAKING BREATH CONTROL A HABIT

What you might be wondering is what the extreme hissing exercise has to do with singing, unless you've got one loooong vowel. So let's work on making sounds and finding out what controlling the release of air adds.

Activity #1

Pick a pitch, any pitch, and sing a long vowel. You can sing an "o" or an "ah." Your goal is to hold out the note as long as you possibly can. Get a stopwatch ready to time yourself.

- On your mark
- Inhale deeply
- Go! "ah"

How long can you hold that note? Ten seconds? Twenty seconds? If you can hold it out for twenty seconds, good job! But did you notice whether or not you took in a deep wide breath to start? Did you notice if you released the air in a strong, steady stream? You've got to pay attention to that every time you sing until it becomes a habit, not just when somebody tells you to pay attention to it. And hopefully paying attention will become a habit pretty quickly.

Activity #2

Here's your 2nd chance on a new vowel, "oh". What do you need to think about?

- On your mark
- Inhale deeply
- Go! "o"

What did you notice? Did you have a steady tone? Maybe it was falling apart toward the end, getting choppy. Did your shoulders sink in? Are you losing that support around your rib cage? How was the sound? Rich and strong, or pinched and meager? If you are giving your vocal folds a steady stream of air, and you aren't pinching the sound off on the way out, it should have sounded pretty good. If you ran out of air – well, it doesn't sound good to squeeze out the last little bit of air. So when you are getting low on air, stop the sound. If it's a long note written in the music but you're out of air, cut the note off. Nobody wants to hear that squeezed sound.

If you're giving your vocal folds a steady stream of air it probably sounds pretty good. In order to sing any song well you've got to be able to count on that steady air or it will be a disappointing experience.

Activity #3

Now we'll try for a deliberately great sound but for a shorter amount of time. Sing your single note for 10 seconds or so.

- Inhale well and keep your core/column strong.
- Ready? Sing.
- Keep your rib cage expanded and your throat mostly relaxed.
- Experiment with different mouth positions to see what your best sound is when you have your breath working right. In other words, change your vowels while you are singing.

Got the idea? You can take it from there. Take a break and work on that for a few minutes. Then come back and we'll do some more.

Next we're going to sing a simple 5-note pattern.

The plan is to inhale with your deep core breath, and control the exhale of air so that you feel that solid column of breath remain intact throughout the exercise. Don't let your rib cage collapse. Don't lean or curl your shoulders forward. Keep a steady, solid posture for all five notes, and all repetitions. You'll pick a starting pitch and after that sing four different pitches that are nearby; perhaps a five note scale. We're going to sing that five-note pattern multiple times with a breath in-between the groups of five. The little inhalation should only replace the air that you've let out. So if you just let out a thimble-full of air, then you're only going to take in a thimble-full of air. Keep your rib cage expanded through the entire exercise. Are you ready to give it a try? Here we go!

Activity #4

- Breathe in fully
- Sing your five-note pattern slowly
- Refill your air for less than a second
- Sing your five-note pattern
- Refill
- Sing your five-note pattern
- Refill
- Sing your five-note pattern
- Refill
- Sing your five-note pattern

- Refill
- Sing your five-note pattern
- Refill

Good! Relax.

> *TIP*
>
> *One professional consideration is how to start (onset) sound if the word starts with a vowel. Some people tend to squeeze their vocal folds for the onset of a vowel word, starting vowel sounds too rough. It is called a glottal onset. A glottal onset always sounds like a little cough or bark at the beginning of a vowel word, like "each." The opposite is an aspirated onset and it sounds like breathy "h's" on vowel words. "(h)Eli (h)eats (h)apples." Got it? Neither one is particularly healthy for your throat. The best thing is called a balanced onset – it is an onset that you can't hear. It should sound like a gentle vowel without a puff of air, and without a tiny cough. You can use the glottal onset when you need to – when it's a stylistic choice, not because you have to and can't do it any differently. As long as you are doing this exercise, pay attention to those onsets and if you have trouble you'll need to spend extra effort on mastering control of onsets.*

Ok, back to work! Repeat the previous exercise until you feel like you have a good grasp of how to take that initial wonderful breath, and keep your "air tanks" (lungs) mostly full while singing several short note patterns (also known as "phrases"). That's how the breathing exercises apply to your singing. When singing, give the sound consistent breath support; not just for slow lines of notes like we've used in these examples, but all the time.

This ends the section on breathing. In the next chapters we'll move on to resonance and alignment of your vocal instrument. Congratulations on your work so far. That was a lot of information and required a lot of processing on your part. If you don't feel ready to move on it is totally fine to jump back to the beginning for a review. Review these chapters several times to develop the best breathing habits.

7 DEVELOPING YOUR UNIQUE SOUND

Some of the breathing exercises that we've done in the first chapters can cause a singer to feel tense or stiff. It's important for a singer to get rid of extra muscle tension. Tension puts a damper on the sound and wear and tear on the voice. The right thing is that a singer's body should actually be loose and flexible, especially if a singer is playing another instrument at the same time.

Think of your body as a musical instrument. You have all of the same components as an instrument. But you have one thing that no other instrument has – your instrument can change shape in a hundred different ways to make an infinite number of different sounds. You can create just about any sound you want, from squeaking like a mouse to howling like a wolf, from beat-box to opera. No other instrument can do that.

Our job in this chapter is to find the position for your body-instrument that makes an easy, sustainable, quality sound. A sound that is "you" - not your musical hero or an imitation of people who sing music you like. We are looking for your unique sound – the sound that makes you stand apart.

For this example I'm going to compare your voice to a trumpet. You have the same source of energy; breath support. Your vocal folds produce the sound in your body instrument. In the trumpet, the sound is produced by the lips against the mouthpiece. The rest of the trumpet produces the rest of the trumpet sound; the sound that is unique to the trumpet.

In the human instrument, it is the shape and size of your vocal folds, and the size and length of the open spaces of your throat and mouth that makes your sound. Those open spaces are the parts you can change, but we'll get to that in a minute.

If you bend the trumpet you get a different sound. Would it be a good sound if you bent the trumpet? Probably not. If you bend your human instrument you're also compromising the sound, and taking the chance of hurting your soft tissue (vocal folds) through misuse.

Activity

- While paying attention to how squished or open your mouth is, honk like a bike-horn. Small, right?
- Next let's go to the opposite – yawn and say "ahhhhh." Huge open space!
- Now, in a regular speech position, sigh "ahhhhh." That is probably a comfortably open, relaxed throat and mouth.

We can't pronounce much when we are that relaxed – we wouldn't be understood. But it is the starting point for a natural sound.

As you go through more vocal exercises and singing songs, remember this feeling of openness and relaxation and apply it as often as you can.

When can you apply it? You can apply it on the vowels. So if you sing something like, "Over the Rainbow," there's a lot of consonants that require you to close your mouth, but the vowels can be long and open. When you're singing those vowels, for most styles of music, you should have the relaxed, open sound.

Now try singing "Over the Rainbow" or another song in a country/western style. You'll still have long vowels, and can still apply some of that relaxed, open mouth, but not quite as much.

> *TIP*
>
> *If you suffer from jaw pain near your ears, you are a prime candidate for jaw relaxation exercises. Talk to your dentist, general practice doctor, or an Ear, Nose, and Throat doctor (ENT) about what you can do to get rid of that pain. There are some non- invasive options; you don't have to live with it.*

Regardless of the style you are performing, from opera to hip-hop, try to do it with as little tension as possible in the mouth and jaw, but still be true to the genre. As a teacher, I have worked with amateur pop, rock, country, and barbershop singers who unconsciously mold-to-death (strangle) their sounds to "blend" or "conform" when the opposite is much better and used by professional singers in every style; to relax and open to create an easy sound. Listen to the best singers in your genre and notice if they sound tight or relaxed. Can you make some of their relaxed (but with supported breath) habits your own?

8 LINING UP THE BODY

Here's a little more about bending that trumpet. The optimal trumpet shape makes the best trumpet sound – it makes sense. In order for you to have the best sound you need the most efficient body position.

And I'm not just talking about neck angle. I'm talking from your toes all the way up. We are going to start at the bottom of you and work to the top to get your whole instrument in the right position.

Toes, why would anyone care about your toes? Well, clench your toes tight. What does that do to your legs? When you clench your toes does that make your legs tight? When your legs are tight does it make your lower back tight? When your lower back is tight it restricts your rib cage; you can't breathe as well.

Activity

1 Stand up straight and tall. Feet hips-width apart, not shoulder-width apart, but hips-width apart.
2 Your feet are strong and spread, your knees are flexible and movable.
3 Do a little wiggle on your knees – feel how they can move.
4 Your hips are slightly tilted forward, tucking your bottom under.
5 Your lower back is loose and flexible. Can you twist and wiggle your lower back a little?

6 Alright, can you twist and turn your whole trunk?

7 Your shoulders?

8 Your chest should be slightly elevated but not so high that it locks your back into place.

9 Make sure your shoulder blades stay loose. That's a tricky one.

10 Your shoulders should be back, down, and relaxed.

11 Your neck – flexible.

12 Check your knees again. Are they still loose? A little bendable?

13 Check your feet. Are they still wide?

14 Lower back, still a little bit wiggly?

15 Okay, back to the flexible neck – that's tricky when singing. A lot of people tense up the back of their neck. So that's one to definitely remember later.

16 For your head, lift the top of your head – the crown. Got it? Maybe you can make yourself a quarter of an inch taller by lifting the top of your head.

17 Elongate your spine. Don't lift your chin. Keep your chin in a nice proud but balanced position.

18 Find a good balance for your head on your spine by gently rocking your head like you're nodding yes. Let it rock slowly, reducing the rocking until you find a balanced position.

19 Check your knees, are they still soft?

20 Check your feet, are they still spread?

21 Your lower back, is it still loose?

22 Are you still tall?

23 And finally, one of the most controlling muscles which interferes with singing - your jaw. Your jaw should be soft

and relaxed. Let it just hang there, like you've got Novocain in your mouth.

You feel strong, solid, well balanced and relaxed.

9 BODY ALIGNMENT WHILE SINGING

Let's jump right in with singing by applying the concepts from the previous section to singing a single note.

Activity

1 Pick an easy note that you can sing for a long time.
2 Take a deep wide breath by expanding your back like a cobra and your torso like a column.
3 Before you sing, are your feet still open? Are your knees still loose? Is your lower back still relaxed, even though you've filled up with breath? Filling up your ribs doesn't mean stiffening your shoulders.
4 In a minute, once you start singing, keep singing. While singing, check your posture and your balance. Breathe whenever you need to and come back in.
5 Now prepare yourself with a good breath to sing your easy note on an "ah" or an "oh."
6 Here we go – sing.
7 Lock and unlock your knees while you're singing. Does this change the sound?
8 Any time that you need to stop and take a breath and start singing again, you go right ahead.
9 Collapse your rib cage while singing. Lift it again. Does that change your sound?

10 Now try changing the angle of your head. Move your chin up and down, side to side. Does that change your sound?
11 Change the angle of your head; rock it gently up and down, side to side.
12 Find the place in your head alignment that sounds the best for your voice. How do we define best? Well, maybe it's the biggest, most relaxed sound. I think you'll know it when you hear it.
13 Finally, while singing your note, tighten your jaw muscles without closing your mouth. Can you clench your jaw while it's open?
14 Then relax your jaw, then tighten again, then relax it. Can you hear the difference when you do that? Even if you can't hear the difference, there's a good chance that a listener could.

You can stop singing now. Did you learn anything interesting? I wish I could have been there to hear it. I bet you found the optimal posture and alignment for your human instrument.

> *TIP*
> *Whenever your voice just doesn't seem to be working the way you want it to, come back to this chapter to check your alignment again.*
> *When you're performing, it would be terrible to be stuck in this neutral position the whole time. That would be a really boring performance. You have to move around and express yourself. Perhaps you perform with an instrument and you have to play the instrument at the same time that you sing. But keep in mind, whatever you do with your body for artistic expression, be as relaxed as possible – not jerky or stiff – and return to this solid*

> *posture and stance for the optimal sound. Make this position the basis for any movement that you do.*

The interesting thing with singing is that the one area that *should not* be relaxed is your breathing muscles. Wow! This is really tough. When else are you expected to be entirely loose in your whole body except your intercostal and abdominal muscles? And how can you be activated and strong in the core of your body and flexible in your lower back? Don't be tempted to clench your jaw and your neck while providing yourself great breath regulation.

Keep your face loose, and keep the strength and energy for your sound coming from the breath muscles of your abdomen and rib cage. These are the kinds of things that singers spend weeks or even months working on in one-to-one voice lessons. It can be done. It takes a lot of practice. It's done all the time by singers who sing well. It's worth paying a lot of attention to.

10 GOOD BODY TENSION

Let's check your body tension. You have found the most relaxed posture possible for the best singing. That means that everything, from your toes to your eyebrows is relaxed, but your breath support in your abs and ribs is strong and activated. You might also remember that completely relaxed singing can make for a really boring performance. It is a fundamental skill that you have to master, so now I'd like to work with you on appropriate tension.

Activity

1 Begin in the standing position and do a rag-doll march to get your energy going. That means do a sloppy march with high knees, but your arms just flopping in a good high swing, for 30 – 60 seconds. Here we go.

2 Next, standing still with feet hips-width apart, check your toes and calves. Are they relaxed? Hips tipped in a little? Lower back soft and relaxed? Shoulders are loose, back, and down? Are your shoulders loose? If not, use activated abs to support your body, not your shoulders. That should help. Next, check your neck – long and tall but soft? Can you swivel your head freely? Finally, relax your face, jaw, and tongue.

3 Now, with passion, say something expressive and positive and see how it affects your posture and tension. Try this: "You are the BEST COOK!" What do you notice? Did your body stay relaxed or did you move? Did it feel natural? For the word "You," your lips came forward, for "are," your jaw dropped. For "best," your mouth spread wide, and "cook" was a more subtle version of "you."
4 Next, your abs. When you say "You are the BEST COOK!" Do you notice your abs tightening?
5 Now let's try singing it with drama. Pick any pitches and sing, "You are the BEST COOK!" It is possible to sing it totally relaxed but boy it loses its passion!
6 Okay, let's mess with it. Tighten your jaw and give it a try; sing, "YOU ARE THE BEST COOK!" What do you think? I felt angry. If you agree then you know an effective way to communicate anger. But say you are one of those people who sings with a tight jaw all of the time. Perhaps you are limiting your expressiveness, limiting your performance, by having a tight jaw.
7 Next, try singing it with a breathy voice, "You are the best cook." For me that is an intimate sound. Nice, but it wouldn't carry very well. I'd need a mic for that expressiveness to carry.

For expression, we naturally add tension. To minimize the tension, try every phrase of any song you are learning by speaking it out loud. Speak it naturally with comfortable expressiveness. Then sing it with the notes without adding new tension – avoid things like a scrunched-up forehead, locked open jaw, stiff neck.

Sometimes we get in such useless habits of tension, tension we don't even know we are using. But if we go too far the other way, too relaxed, our performance becomes lifeless. So use tension consciously and deliberately.

Watch yourself sing in a mirror. You might be surprised at what you see.

11 BAD BODY TENSION

There are some common bad singing tensions that all singers should be aware of. We see them all the time in amateur singers and sometimes in professionals. Bad tensions can take away from a performance.

They can be distracting, make for a lower quality sound, and if used often enough and long enough, can cause harm.

There are many possible bad tensions. They can be in the face, tongue, jaw, neck, throat, shoulders, and body. But some of them are more common than others. Here are three tensions that we see in many armature singers:

> - *Leaning forward at the hips*
> - *Stretching the neck forward*
> - *Noisy breathing*

First is leaning forward at the hips. It has an effect on the voice – it changes the throat and decreases breath control. It also has a major effect on how the singer looks. What often happens is the singer will be standing in a wonderful, relaxed, calm posture, but as they take the first breath of the song in a gasping way, they also lean forward. A good way to test out if you have this problem is by standing up against a flat wall. Find your comfortable posture for singing against the wall. Pick a song to break into – you will only need one phrase. As soon as you are ready, inhale and begin singing. If you find yourself moving forward, then you have some tension habits to break. If this is a problem for you, the first thing to remember is how to fill your lungs (as covered in chapters two through six). Next you need to break the habit of leaning forward. You can practice singing against the wall regularly to check your progress.

Second bad tension habit – stretching forward or up at the neck. This has a direct effect on the quality of your sound, accuracy of your pitch, and it affects your appearance. We often don't realize we are doing this because as soon as we start singing our mind leaves thoughts of posture behind. The key is to remember the feeling of a balanced head. Rest one hand gently on your jaw or chin and the other on the back of your neck. Get ready to sing your song. Feel for your head tipping up or forward. If you have this bad habit, you will have to break it or you will never have a relaxed, natural sound, and you will never be able to rely on your pitch accuracy. Sing a complete song with this in mind. If you found your chin going up you'll need to fix this bad habit.

Common ways to work with a singer to eliminate this habit is to have a singer roll their neck while singing, sing bent over at the waist, or draped over a yoga ball. Hand-held neck massagers can also be useful in relaxing the muscles.

The last common tension to cover is noisy breathing. That is, when you take air in we can hear it. In our everyday lives, most of us breathe almost silently.

Even when instructed to take a deep breath, we usually have a wide open throat and the breath is pretty quiet. But for most people, as soon as they breath for singing, they forget to have that wide open throat. You will rarely hear noisy breathing on commercial CDs. One of the jobs of the recording engineer is to take out the breath noises. But you can't believe how common noisy breathing is. The problem is that a tight throat during the intake of air means your throat can't be relaxed when you are singing, so the sound will be tight, your resonance will be reduced, and your audience might be distracted. The better choice, a loose, open throat during inhalation, means the singer has all of their options open to them when it comes to creating sound.

Bookmark this chapter and return to it over and over. Most of us can name professional singers in just about any genre who are very tense. But do you respect them for that tension? Probably not. And that tension can land a singer in a doctor's chair, having caused temporary or chronic hoarseness.

> *TIP*
>
> *Two tension related rules every singer must live by:*
>
> - *If it hurts, don't do it.*
> - *If it makes you hoarse then something is wrong.*

12 VOICE CLASSIFICATIONS AND REGISTRATION

Classifications means labeling your voice type by optimal pitch range and character. There are at least two different worlds of classifications for singers; classical and non-classical. First I'll explain the classifications for many styles of music. Men are divided into three main categories. Those categories are bass (the lowest), baritone (this is the most common, typical male range), and tenor (or lead). The majority of men's songs in pop and rock are written in the tenor range. Country seems to give more opportunities baritones than other genres do. Women usually divide as alto (the lowest) and soprano (the highest). Sopranos seem to be slightly more common among professionals.

For classification in classical solo and choral singing, the divisions are similar. Most choruses are divided, from lowest to highest, into baritones, tenors, altos and sopranos. But in opera, and specifically in the German Fach system, (fach means "type" or "compartment"), the voice types are expanded out to Bass, Bass-Baritone, Baritone, Tenor, Countertenor, Contralto, Mezzo-soprano and Soprano. Additionally, those categories are divided into subcategories such as "dramatic soprano" or "lyric soprano", "tenor buffo" or "heldentenor." There are approximately 24 subdivisions. In the world of choral music, a singer in the alto section would usually be called a mezzo-soprano in classical music. A female tenor would be called a contralto in opera.

If you are wondering what your voice classification is, you might use tools on the internet or apps that will identify your voice type. They will classify your voice by determining your lowest notes and highest notes. But this is only a part of the formula for determining voice type. We also consider where the breaks are and what the color of the sound is. To get a good idea of voice type, a singer needs to work a series of vocal exercises with a knowledgeable choir director or voice teacher.

Registration is a separate issue from Classification.

Generally tone colors, or voice qualities, are known as registration. Registration has to do with how heavy or light a sound is, how driven or relaxed, how loud, or how much breath pressure. Registration is tied closely to emotional expression - listeners get emotioinal "messages," telling them how the singer feels, through registration choices. There are many different names but some common ones are belting, speech-like, and legit, chest voice, head voice, and mix.

Belting is tricky to define because it sounds different in different genres, and can be described and produced differently depending on the pitch range comfort for that singer. But essentially, belting is anything that is loud and often piercing, and packed with emotional energy..

Speech-like is conversational singing. It requires a mic for amplification.

The term *legit* is used for gentle, smooth singing for women and often means high range notes. Similarly, *falsetto* for men can be found at the highest part of the voice but the word falsetto is going out of favor as it has negative connotations, as if it always sounds weak and breathy. Instead, men who comfortably sing near the top of their range (like Bruno Mars, Barry Gibb, and others), often call it their *high voice.* All men have a high voice (or falsetto), regardless of voice type. The terms *high voice, head voice*, and *legit*, for women, are interchangeable. For men, the words *high voice, falsetto*, and sometimes *head voice*, are interchangeable. Legit is short for *legitimate* and falsetto is Italian for *little false.* Isn't it interesting that the very names of these natural and ubiquitous parts of the human voice are biased.

Finally, the highest pitch range is whistle tone, or whistle register. Whistle tone is at the very top of the female or male voice. Many people, no matter the voice type, can make a few notes up there with practice but there is very, very little practical reason to do so. Arianna Grande and Mariah Carey have found ways to make whistle tone part of their performances. The Guinness world record holder for the highest note, in whistle tone, is a man named Amirhossein Molaei (July 2019, singing an F#8 at 5989 Hz).

What do all of these registration labels mean for a singer? All singers should learn to control their belting, speech-like, smooth, and high voice singing styles, and be able to switch between them comfortably in a coordinated way. This skill is essential to being good story-tellers and accomplished singers. For most untrained singers one part of your voice is much, much stronger than other parts. That would generally be the part of your voice that you use for speaking.

Confused? I don't blame you. There are so many names for different singing qualities, and many of them overlap. Even among voice teachers, there isn't complete consensus about common terms that pretty much mean the same thing, like the near-synonyms head voice, high voice, falsetto, legit, treble, voce di testa, and cricothyroid dominant (CT). All of those labels refer to general pitch ranges, but once we also consider tone quality and loudness, the waters get even more muddy.

Nonetheless, registration is a big part of studying singing. We can't shy away from it, so let's dive in, muddy or not.

Activity

- Let’s try registration out a little to discover what we’re talking about. In a low, rich, strong sound, say a loud “Hello!” Next, turn that into singing. Does this feel like it is in your natural speaking voice? For many people it will. When you sing or speak this, you might feel vibrations in your chest. That is why it is frequently called your chest voice. There's actually no sound-making going on in your chest, but there is some nice, lively sensation there.

- Now let's try it in the gentle, high part of your voice, men and women both. You can go very high for this, but please don't go into a small, cartoony voice. Keep it big and full; like Julia Child might have used. Speak “Hello.” Now sing “Hello.” There will be some who will have a hard time with this because they've never developed the muscles that control these pitches. If you can't find the high notes and it comes out more like a belt or yell, then you will want to spend practice time developing this part of your voice. This part of your voice is often called your head voice. The higher you go into your head voice, the more likely you will feel the resonant vibrations in parts of your head.

- Now we'll do a shift from one voice to the next. Start on a low chest-voice note, and slide all the way up to your highest high-voice (or head-voice, or falsetto) note. Did you hear a little break? In classical singing that is called your *passaggio* and in English we call it a *break*, but I like to call it a *speed bump*. People often bounce right over it. If you plan well you might not hear it and if you slam into it too fast or heavy, there's no telling where it will land. In some styles, like in yodeling, it is important to emphasize the break.

- Turn it around and start from the top – from your highest note. Slide down to your lowest note. How did it go? For some people it's easy, for others it is extraordinarily difficult. It depends on how you are put together and what muscle strengths and coordination you have. But there's hope for everyone to have control of it if you put in some time and effort.

You'll find great exercises to improve your registration transition at: nancybos.me/media

13 USING RESONANCE TO ENHANCE SINGING

Resonance is defined as:
a: the intensification and enriching of a musical tone by supplementary vibration
b: a quality imparted to voiced sounds by vibration in anatomical resonating chambers or cavities (such as the mouth or the nasal cavity)
c: a quality of richness or variety

"resonance," Merriam-Webster.com Dictionary, https://www.merriam-webster.com/dictionary/resonance.

To put it in everyday words, resonance means how sound waves bounce around on their way out of your mouth.

Opera singers use the biggest resonance possible to fill the hall and sing over the orchestra without mics. Folk singers often use a very small resonance to create an intimate sound. They must use mics to be heard over instruments and in large rooms. Most other styles use a combination of different resonances, sometimes in the same song.

Sometimes people think they have one, true sound – one authentic resonance that they identify with. But this is ridiculously limiting. If you are shouting across a football field, you use a big space in your mouth and project the sound like a megaphone. Give it a try. Yell "hey" as loud as you can. Was your mouth wide open? That is very different from whispering where you have a small mouth and keep the vibrations in the middle mouth area. Give that a try with a quiet, "hey."

So if you don't limit your speaking to one kind, why would you limit your singing? Anyone can sing with a big, open mouth one minute and with a small, closed mouth the next. In other words, anyone can maximize their resonance or minimize their resonance for what the song needs.

Activity

As you've already read, mouth shape has a lot to do with it. Let's experiment with this.

1. Repeat a hoot 3 times. Make it big (hoo – hoo – hoooo). Now make it small (hoo – hoo – hoooo).
2. Next we are going to hold out a long "oo" and experiment with different resonance on that one vowel. Take a breath whenever you need to and come back in. Start by making a nice, neutral, middle-of-the-mouth "oo." Your tongue is down, the roof of your mouth is up.
3. Now move that resonance forward, like it's right on your lips and teeth. Do this by making your mouth smaller in the back – squishing the sound forward. It might help if I say to make it very bright. Or perhaps if I say to feel like you are focusing your air toward your nose.
4. Next we are going to send the sound toward the back. Go back to the middle of the mouth "oo," with the lowered tongue and raised roof. Put your hands behind your neck and interlock your fingers. Visualize sending the sound back to your hands. It probably means opening the back of your mouth and throat

more. This might sound like an opera sound or maybe even a swallowed sound.

5 Next put the interlocked hands on top of your head. Can you send the sound up to them? This is a nice tall sound. This is my personal favorite place to visualize the resonance. It feels like I'm getting a brain massage and the sound is nice and big. However it isn't the right sound for a lot of styles. A punk singer or a crooner would rarely want this sound. So pick the type of resonance that is good for the song you are singing.

Listen to some of the most respected and creative singers; Dave Matthews, Joni Mitchell, Celine Dion, Aretha Franklin, Kristin Chenoweth, Nat King Cole, Bruno Mars, and Reba McEntire to name a few. You'll hear that they use a wide variety of resonances. They use them for expressiveness, for emotion.

In general, choose the resonance that feels "natural" but don't be afraid to experiment with different types of resonance. Is there a "right" kind of sound? No, the music tells you the emotions to use and the emotions tell you what kind of resonance to use. If you are using a mic, don't worry about projecting as much. If you won't have a mic, use a bigger space in your vocal tract, which is your mouth and throat, to maximize your resonance.

Resonance is a difficult topic to cover in print. I'm sorry to admit that. It is definitely a topic to explore extensively in one-to-one voice lessons with a singing teacher or coach. If you'd like more on this topic outside of lessons, I encourage you to check out the 35 minute long *Singing 101: Resonance* class at nancybos.me/courses. Use the coupon **101Book** for $10 (USD) off the class.

14 NOTE STYLES AND DIPHTHONGS

Note Style: A big part of style can be heard in how the singer connects the notes. There are countless options, but the two extremes are *legato* and *staccato*.

> *Legato – smooth notes*
>
> *Staccato – choppy or bouncy notes.*

At the beginning of a song, before taking a full breath and getting a nice balanced onset, you will have to choose *staccato, legato*, or someplace in between.

Smooth singing, aka *legato* - The breath needs to carry you through the whole phrase with measured, smooth control, connecting one note to the next as long as it is right for the song. *Legato* might include sliding between pitches.

Bouncy singing, aka *staccato* – The breath still needs to take you through the whole phrase with measured control, but this time the notes are not connected – there will be a little space in-between notes. If you are singing *staccato* on a word that begins with a vowel remember your onsets – not too harsh, not too breathy – balanced onsets. If you want a review of onsets, see Chapter 6. *Staccato* will require nailing the exact pitch at the onset, without scoops or slides.

Considering the style of music is important. The way we connect our notes helps us define the style we are singing in.

Word Pronunciation: Another consideration is word pronunciation - specifically diphthongs. Diphthongs are words that contain two vowel sounds together. There's also such a thing as triphthongs – that is 3 vowel sounds together as in "our" – "ah-o-oo-er."

Vowel pronunciation is a dead give-away of a regional accent and is very import when deciding on the style of a song. Let me give you an example in the word "play." When you say "play" you hear 2 clear vowel sounds - "a" and "e" "Pla-ey." When you sing the word "play" on a long note you have to choose how to switch from the first vowel sound to the second vowel sound. Is the "a" longer, the "e" longer, or are they equal? (sing "Plaaaaae, Plaeeeee, Plaaaeee") Can you think of other diphthongs? Eye, Care, Phone, Babe, Blind. And there are many more.

As a general rule, classical singing draws out the first vowel sound (sing babe like this: "Baaaaaebe), country singing draws out the second vowel ("Baeeeeebe") and popular music has balanced vowel sounds ("Baaeebe"). So if you are switching back and forth, say in a choir, between a classical song and a popular or folk song, notice how you will pronounce them differently.

21-DAY ACTION PLAN AND JOURNAL

An essential aspect of becoming a better singer is singing every day. Just like any muscle group, the voice needs to be toned and strengthened. And to make new techniques become a habit, they need to be repeated over and over.

In this chapter you have the opportunity to write your vocal activity every day for twenty-one days. Log your reading, the amount of time spent doing warm-ups, exercises, and songs. There is even a "Bonus" category for days that you do extra singing outside of practice.

Snap a picture of your 21-Day Action Plan and share it with me on Instagram (singing101vocalbasics) or Facebook (Nancy Bos Voice Studio). I would love to hear what a difference this daily vocal workout is making for your singing!

Definitions

Warm-Ups: The act of preparing to sing by doing gentle physical and vocal stretches, targeting breathing, pitch range, physical freedom, lips, and tongue. Warm-ups include slides and lip trills, breathing exercises, marching in place, buzzing lips, and trilling the tongue among other things. Warm-ups can take as little as five minutes.

Exercises: Vocal work designed to tone and strengthen the voice, utilizing the best possible technique. The best exercises are custom designed in a one-on-one coaching session with a voice teacher. **There are also many exercies available at NancyBos.me/media**

Directions

For each of 21 days, including weekends, find at least twenty-five minutes to sing and ten minutes to read.

Review Singing 101 each day, and add other readings from blogs and articles, or other on-line and print resources. The more you know the faster you can grow.

Plan on five minutes of warm-ups. Many of the breathing, posture, and pitch sliding exercises make good warm-ups. Add tongue trills and lip buzzes to get everything going.

Take advantage of the free exercises at nancybos.me/media. Exercises are where most of the change comes in. Pick an area to target, such as breath control or range strengthening. Spend 10 – 20 minutes working on improving your skills in this area.

You can sing any song you would like. Use it as an opportunity to apply the skills from your exercises to a real song that you might perform.

The Bonus category is to list any additional singing outside of practice, such as choir rehearsal, singing in the car, or a band rehearsal.

You hear and feel a difference in your voice in as little as five days. By fourteen days, the new skills will be becoming habits. By twenty-one days you will have a deeper understanding of your voice, your gifts, and what areas you would like to continue working on. But don't stop there – it only takes a couple of days to have a decrease in muscle tone. Stick with it! Your voice will be stronger, healthier, and more like the voice you dream of having!

DATE ____ DAY# ____ 21-Day Action Plan

READING: ____________________

WARM-UPS: ____________________

EXERCISES: ____________________

SONGS: ____________________

BONUS: ____________________

Journal: ____________________

____

____

____

DATE ____ DAY# ____ 21-Day Action Plan

READING: ____________________

WARM-UPS: ____________________

EXERCISES: ____________________

SONGS: ____________________

BONUS: ____________________

Journal: ____________________

____

____

____

DATE ____ DAY# ____ 21-Day Action Plan

READING: ______________________________

WARM-UPS: ______________________________

EXERCISES: ______________________________

SONGS: ______________________________

BONUS: ______________________________

Journal: ______________________________

____

____

____

DATE ____ DAY# ____ 21-Day Action Plan

READING: ______________________________

WARM-UPS: ______________________________

EXERCISES: ______________________________

SONGS: ______________________________

BONUS: ______________________________

Journal: ______________________________

____

____

____

DATE ____ DAY# ____ 21-Day Action Plan

READING: ______________________________

WARM-UPS: ______________________________

EXERCISES: ______________________________

SONGS: ______________________________

BONUS: ______________________________

Journal: ______________________________

____

____

____

DATE ____ DAY# ____ 21-Day Action Plan

READING: ______________________________

WARM-UPS: ______________________________

EXERCISES: ______________________________

SONGS: ______________________________

BONUS: ______________________________

Journal: ______________________________

____

____

____

DATE ____ DAY# ____ 21-Day Action Plan

READING: ____________________

WARM-UPS: ____________________

EXERCISES: ____________________

SONGS: ____________________

BONUS: ____________________

Journal: ____________________

____

____

____

DATE ____ DAY# ____ 21-Day Action Plan

READING: ____________________

WARM-UPS: ____________________

EXERCISES: ____________________

SONGS: ____________________

BONUS: ____________________

Journal: ____________________

____

____

____

DATE ____ DAY# ____ 21-Day Action Plan

READING: ________________________________

WARM-UPS: ________________________________

EXERCISES: ________________________________

SONGS: ________________________________

BONUS: ________________________________

Journal: ________________________________

____

____

____

DATE ____ DAY# ____ 21-Day Action Plan

READING: ________________________________

WARM-UPS: ________________________________

EXERCISES: ________________________________

SONGS: ________________________________

BONUS: ________________________________

Journal: ________________________________

____

____

____

DATE ____ DAY# ____ 21-Day Action Plan

READING: ____________________

WARM-UPS: ____________________

EXERCISES: ____________________

SONGS: ____________________

BONUS: ____________________

Journal: ____________________

DATE ____ DAY# ____ 21-Day Action Plan

READING: ____________________

WARM-UPS: ____________________

EXERCISES: ____________________

SONGS: ____________________

BONUS: ____________________

Journal: ____________________

DATE ____ DAY# ____ 21-Day Action Plan

READING: ____

WARM-UPS: ____

EXERCISES: ____

SONGS: ____

BONUS: ____

Journal: ____

____

____

____

DATE ____ DAY# ____ 21-Day Action Plan

READING: ____

WARM-UPS: ____

EXERCISES: ____

SONGS: ____

BONUS: ____

Journal: ____

____

____

____

DATE ____ DAY# ____ 21-Day Action Plan

READING: ____________________

WARM-UPS: ____________________

EXERCISES: ____________________

SONGS: ____________________

BONUS: ____________________

Journal: ____________________

DATE ____ DAY# ____ 21-Day Action Plan

READING: ____________________

WARM-UPS: ____________________

EXERCISES: ____________________

SONGS: ____________________

BONUS: ____________________

Journal: ____________________

DATE ____ DAY# ____ 21-Day Action Plan

READING: ______________________________

WARM-UPS: ______________________________

EXERCISES: ______________________________

SONGS: ______________________________

BONUS: ______________________________

Journal: ______________________________

____

____

____

DATE ____ DAY# ____ 21-Day Action Plan

READING: ______________________________

WARM-UPS: ______________________________

EXERCISES: ______________________________

SONGS: ______________________________

BONUS: ______________________________

Journal: ______________________________

____

____

____

DATE ____ DAY# ____ 21-Day Action Plan

READING: ____________________

WARM-UPS: ____________________

EXERCISES: ____________________

SONGS: ____________________

BONUS: ____________________

Journal: ____________________

____

____

____

DATE ____ DAY# ____ 21-Day Action Plan

READING: ____________________

WARM-UPS: ____________________

EXERCISES: ____________________

SONGS: ____________________

BONUS: ____________________

Journal: ____________________

____

____

____

DATE ____ DAY# ____ 21-Day Action Plan

READING: ____________________

WARM-UPS: ____________________

EXERCISES: ____________________

SONGS: ____________________

BONUS: ____________________

Journal: ____________________

____

____

____

Congratulations! You Did It!
Enjoy your new vocal skills,
review this book regularly, and
shoot for your next singing goal!

CONCLUSION

Singing 101: Vocal Basics and Fundamental Singing Skills for All Styles and Abilities is a great introduction to singing lessons. You have been exposed to a large amount of information and it will take repetition and reinforcement to form the new habits you will need.

Breathing, tension, relaxation, alignment, resonance, classification, registration, pronunciation, and much more, are details that every singer who studies voice learns about and masters in voice lessons. It is fair to say that nearly every voice teacher has a slightly different way of communicating very similar concepts, and unfortunately, some of us have very different concepts, based in erroneous tradition rather than science. The study of voice science is a rapidly growning field as we gain ways to observe the voice muscles in action, and analyze the data.

But don't let the varying opinions and new science discourage you. Every individual can benefit from getting to know their singing voice better, and gaining skills in performing.

I hope this book is an inspiration to you to continue your vocal study. Seek out a teacher through reputable organizations such as NATS.org or ask for recommendations from singers in your community. Take sample lessons with a few teachers to find who fits your style the best. Consider online, distance voice lessons – they are a great and convenient way to study with a quality teacher. Use this opportunity to grow the passion for singing which you have harbored your whole life.

"If I cannot fly, let me sing." – Stephen Sondheim

For singing exercises and resources, such as Nancy's podcasts and blogs, visit NancyBos.me. Sign up for Nancy's mailing list so you won't miss a single podcast episode or new exercise posting.

Cantar 101: Principios vocales y destrezas fundamentales de canto para todos los estil is the Spanish language version of Singing 101. It is a direct, word for word translation, tremendously useful for Spanish speaking singers and for bi-lingual group classes and choir. Available in print, kindle, and audiobook.

The Teen Girl's Singing Guide: Tips for Making Singing the Focus of Your Life. Nancy Bos speaks real to teen girls about how to BE a singer. This illustrated book and journal lets teens explore all of the options including (and way beyond) being a pop star or professional singer. This is also a book for parents who want to understand the complex and vital relationship of emotional health, career training, and singing and how singing empowers our daughters. *The Teen Girl's Singing Guide* is personal, profound, and practical!

Singing Through Change: Women's Voices in Midlife, Menopause, and Beyond, is the highly acclaimed, Amazon bestselling book for women who sing, as well as their singing teachers, choral directors, speech therapists, and ENTs.

Written by women for women, this compelling and easy to read book is a collection of unique lived singing experiences from every stage in an adult woman's life combined with the science needed for women and their singing mentors to decipher singing issues.

Singer's Practice Plan, Log and Journal: A Planner for Singing Students is a one of a kind tool designed exclusively for singers by a voice teacher and students. Available in navy, purple, red, green and white on singersplanner.com. It is a must-have for any singing student from middle school thru college.

ABOUT THE AUTHOR

Nancy Bos has been a voice teacher since 1995, when, under the guidance of her mentor, Dr. Candace Magner, University of New Mexico, Nancy began a career that has allowed her to help thousands of singers explore their love for singing. It also allowed her to raise her two children with a good balance between parenting and her career – a win/win!

Nancy's journey as a vocal pedagogue has included mentors Robert Edwin and Ute Freund. Nancy benefitted from the NATS Internship in 2005, studying with Robert Edwin and Dr. Scott McCoy. Since the original publication of Singing 101 in 2006, she has received the Distinguished Voice Professional certification from the New York Singing Teachers Association, and she has taught at Cornish College of the Arts, Seattle Pacific University, and Bellevue College. She also served for six years on the board of the National Association of Teachers of Singing (NATS).

Nancy is an in demand speaker on freeing the voice. She also loves to sing and play in groups – from rock and contemporary bands, to a cappella and bluegrass. Nancy has performed in, and music directed for, several musicals. She has enjoyed touring in Europe and South America with her church choir, and is a frequent soloist at her church.

Nancy's hobbies include gardening, biking, voiceover acting, and traveling to sunny places from her home outside of Seattle, Washington.

Made in the USA
Las Vegas, NV
18 December 2023